MW01105862

LIFE EDUCATION

Living in the World

Written by Kate Cann
Illustrated by Derek Matthews

FRANKLIN WATTS
A Division of Grolier Publishing
NEW YORK • LONDON • HONG KONG • SYDNEY
DANBURY, CONNECTICUT

First American Edition 1997 by
Franklin Watts
A Division of Grolier Publishing
Sherman Turnpike
Danbury, CT 06816

10 9 8 7 6 5 4 3 2 1

Cann, Kate.
    Living in the world / Kate Cann.
       p. cm. — (Life education)
    Includes index.
    Summary: Uses case histories to discuss a
person's place in the world and his or her
relationship with other people and the
environment.
    ISBN 0-531-14430-5
    1. Adjustment (Psychology)—Case studies.
2. Interpersonal conflict. 3. Self-management
(Psychology). [1. Interpersonal relations. 2. Conduct
of life.] I. Title. II. Series.
BF335.C36 1997
158'.2—dc20
                                    96-11877
                                    CIP AC

Edited by: Helen Lanz
Designed by: Sally Boothroyd
Commissioned photography by:
Peter Millard
Illustrations by: Derek Matthews

Printed in Italy

Acknowledgments:
Commissioned photography by Peter Millard: cover; title
page.
Researched photography: Eye Ubiqitious 11 (Skjold), 16
(Skjold), 23 (J. Burke); Franklin Watts CD transparency;
Sally and Richard Greenhills 19; Hulton Getty 21; The
Hutchinson Library 12; John Walmsley 26; Magnum 10
(J. Nachtwey); Panos 27 (E. Miller); Photofusion 4 (S.
Lancaster); Ronald Grant 24 ("Mad Max II"/1981,
Kennedy Miller Productions/Columbia - EMI - Warner
Distributors); Tony Stone 17 (B. Ayres), 29 (D. Wolff).
Artwork: Cartoon illustrations by Derek Matthews
throughout.

The publishers wish to acknowledge that the
photographs reproduced in this book have
been posed by models or obtained from
photographic picture agencies.

Franklin Watts and Life Education
International are indebted to Susan Kaplin,
Amanda Friend, Vince Hatton, and Laurie
Noffs for their invaluable help.

Franklin Watts would like to extend their
special thanks to all the actors who appear
in the Life Education books:

Hester Cann   Giles Farnham
James Ceppi di Lecco   Howard Newton
James Chandler   Miles Newton
Chloe Parsons   Amelia Wood
Dipali Patel   Andrew Wood

*'Each second we live is a new and unique moment of the universe, a moment
that will never be again...And what do we teach our children? We teach
them that two and two make four and that Paris is the capital of France.*

*When will we also teach them: do you know who you are? You are a marvel.
You are unique. In all the years that have passed, there has never been
another child like you. And look at your body – what a wonder it is! Your
legs, your arms, your clever fingers, the way you move. You may become a
Shakespeare, a Michelangelo, a Beethoven. You have the capacity for
anything. Yes, you are a marvel. And when you grow up, can you then harm
another who is, like you, a marvel? You must cherish one another. You must
work – we must all work – to make this world worthy of its children.'*

Pablo Casals

A famous Spanish musician, also noted for his humanitarian beliefs.
(1876 - 1973)

CONTENTS

Get ready to use your brains and expand your minds. We're going to look at YOU in the world.

THE SPIRAL EFFECT

No one else in your life is as important as you. You are vital, the center of your world. If you're not OK, nothing else in your world can be OK. Because of this, you have a strong responsibility toward yourself. In a real sense, you come first. You must respect yourself, take care of yourself, and protect yourself. You must do what you can to grow and develop so that you can reach your full potential.

MAKING CONNECTIONS

But you don't live in a vacuum, and you can't survive in a box. The things you do and the way you behave have an effect, not only on you, but on everyone else around you. You may think you're isolated and on your own — but in fact you're always connected to other people. You may think what you do doesn't matter to anyone else but you — but it does! Your actions COUNT.

And this is where the good part comes in. When you behave in a way that adds something useful to the world around you, you often find it adds something good to your life, too. It's a two-way process. It's not only the big things that matter, either. It's the little ones as well. Little things can build into something important.

Good things often lead to more good things, while bad things can lead to worse. It's an ACCUMULATIVE effect.

Some ways of hanging out, help out!

Hold on there, let me check my data. Oh, yes, ACCUMULATIVE: gathering together in an increasing quantity; amassing; collecting.

SPIRAL UP, SPIRAL DOWN...

It's like a spiral going up and up, with good things leading to more good things; or a spiral heading down and down, going from bad to worse. To climb up, or to slide down, is a daily choice. Which will you go for?

YOU AND OTHERS

Friendships and good family relationships take effort, just like taking care of yourself takes effort. The trick is not to see any of it as hard work, but as something you can find pleasure in. And efforts usually are rewarded in some way — a healthier body, happier home life, closer friends — bringing you more pleasure and fulfillment. The more times you make these simple efforts, the easier it gets, and the better life becomes. It's the upward spiral taking effect.

ONE SMALL STEP...

Upward spirals?! Making efforts? Are you kidding? My life is a disaster! Everything's gone wrong! What's the point of trying? My LIFE just went down the drain!

Hang on, hang on — calm down. Cut the drama. Life gets out of control for everyone at times. But there's NEARLY ALWAYS something you can do. The trick is to turn the disaster around slowly — by taking one small step forward, then another, however defeated you feel. It may seem like there's a great mountain ahead of you that you'll never have the courage to climb — but don't let the mountain overwhelm you. Try to figure out what the first step is, and then make it. You'll be surprised how you speed up once the spiral effect gets going!

IS THERE ANYBODY THERE?

Another trick is to remember that there are people out there! When you need help, try to *ask for it*: from friends, from family, from teachers at school. Knock on doors, phone, write, talk, scream; someone might listen to you. Someone might even be able to help. Whereas if you go all defeatist, and lock yourself away from everyone, no one will know you need help.

The secret is in my coding! I take one step at a time, and whenever I can't operate on my own, I whiz down the Internet and ASK FOR HELP!

! *SLIDING BACK*
When times are bad, one of the worst decisions you can make is to think that getting into alcohol or drugs will take your mind off your problems, or help you to cope. Going for either of these options will just create another huge problem for you to solve — probably a lot worse than the first one!

CASE HISTORY

Tom's Information Technology teacher knew she could trust him — he was one of her best pupils — so when Tom asked if he could stay late in the lab to work on his project, she was happy to agree. "Just don't delete my master file!" she'd joked.

Some joke. Tom started playing around, moving text about — and forgot to save the original file. AAAAAAGH!

Tom's first thought was to throw himself out of the window. He knew just how long that master file had taken to put together, how many kids had stuff on it.... That night he crawled home, overwhelmed with depression.

His dad got the whole story out of him. "I can't go back to school," Tom said. But Tom's dad persuaded him he'd have to. "You've got to tell your teacher, pal. If you hide from her, things'll get worse and

worse. She might even be able to help."

So Tom did. And as Tom had feared, his teacher was furious. But as she strode off to the lab, Tom had to admit he felt slightly better. He felt he'd faced up to something.

The next day his teacher told him he would have to go back to each of the student's own files and, one by one, copy all the relevant parts over. Then she smiled and told him that she did understand — mistakes happen to everybody. Tom worked every evening for the rest of that week. It was hard work, but better than worrying about it, and certainly better than jumping out of the window.

SMALL ACTIONS MAKE A BIG DIFFERENCE

1. Your room is a dump — it's past help. It will take you two weeks and a bulldozer to clean it.

2. You're too depressed to do anything more than just pick up those clothes over there...

3. and take the dirty cups downstairs before you get yelled at...

4. then you may as well make the bed...

5. dump the garbage...

6. OK, cancel the bulldozer!

INFLUENCE YOUR OWN REALITY

You are a magician. You can conjure up many of the things you want in your life. It's all to do with attitude. That's not just making the best of things, looking on the bright side — although that can certainly help. It's actually influencing what happens to you, how people treat you and react to you — just by the way you behave.

ATTRACTING YOUR OWN LIFE

It's a do-it-yourself life we're all in. Although it's a fact that some people start out with far greater advantages than others, it's also a fact that you can start out with very little, yet become very successful. Or you can start out with loads of advantages and still end up a sad case! It's all to do with how you interact with the world around you. Like a type of magnet, you attract your own life.

HOW TO MAKE YOUR OWN PARTY

CASE HISTORY: CURES FOR BOREDOM

Jane, Greg, and Matt always complained that nothing exciting ever happened to them. They moaned about how boring their town and school was. They made being bored into an art form.

Then Matt met some new friends. They said they'd solved the problem of being bored. They used inhalants — anything that gave them an artificial buzz. "It gets us away from all this. Try it."

So Jane and Greg did, but they didn't enjoy the trip very much. Jane felt sick and dizzy, Greg felt panicky. "You've got to stick to it," Matt's new friends said. "You'll get used to it."

Jane and Greg didn't want to get used to it. Matt was used to it and he'd started acting really strange — suddenly flaring up at them, slurring his words. And he was looking worse and worse. He had all these little sores around his mouth.

Jane and Greg's attitude to boredom changed. "Maybe things weren't quite as boring before as we thought," Greg said. "And look at Matt! I'm worried about him!"

Jane nodded. "You're right. I've kind of figured out that it's up to us to make the most of things. I, uh, called in at the sports center on the way home. There are loads of things coming up that we could get involved with."

"What about Matt? What should we do about him?"

"Yeah, Matt," said Jane. "He needs help." They spoke to a teacher at school who had also noticed Matt's problem and he *was* helped — before it was too late.

VIRTUAL VERSUS REALITY

OK, OK, it's riveting. In soaps, life is always full of action. That's because a scriptwriter made it all up! You might think your family is dull and your friends are so-so, but they're real. Other people's lives might seem far more glamorous and exciting than yours, but life on the screen is a substitute for reality. Just watching them and envying them has to be more boring than even the most boring event in your life. Try talking to the people around you. Start living your life!

If life was really like that — with deaths, divorces, and dramas all the time, and long-lost relatives turning up every other day — you'd go crazy!

JUST WHAT IS IT WITH SOME PEOPLE?

Well, just what is it with some people? Why do they behave in such a rotten way? Is it something they choose to do? Do they decide to be bad because they enjoy it?

Or don't they have any choice? Were they made that way because of bad things that happened to them? Were they even BORN that way?

It's all very well to go on about being positive and reaching out and... what was it... interacting?

Oh yes! To interact — to act in close relation with. That's something I know all about! Think of it, if my drive didn't interact with other computers, then...

Yeah, yeah... People are different though! Some people I wouldn't even want to get within a mile of, let alone act "in close relation with." Face it. Some people are THE PITS.

NATURE – NURTURE – FREE WILL – NATURE ...

The nature-versus-nurture debate began with the ancient philosophers and goes on and on. Were we *born* the way we are, as part of nature, or *made* the way we are, because of our upbringing, or nurturing? And where does free will — the idea that you can choose to do good or bad — fit into all this?

Some people used to think that children were bad by nature. They had to be raised very strictly for their own good.

Then we began to think experience made you what you are. If you had a brutal father and a drunken mother — how could you be good?

It wasn't your fault you went off the deep end. It was the fault of your circumstances, of society. You can imagine how neat an excuse that can be sometimes.

Perhaps the truth is more complex. Perhaps people are made up of parts of nature and nurture, and one more important element: the fact that they can make choices! How much do you think what you are today is due to the character you were born with, and how much is due to your experiences of life so far?

Burning ambition — where will it get them?

CASE HISTORY

Claire's life was getting tougher and tougher. Her dad had walked out, her older brother was always in trouble with the police, and her mom just couldn't cope any more.

Claire and Lucy had been friends for years, but now Lucy's mother wanted to put a stop to the friendship. She thought Claire was a "bad influence." Claire would get drunk and wreck things. She sometimes smoked dope and shoplifted.

Lucy hated how Claire behaved, but she understood it: Claire sometimes acted as though she didn't care about her own survival simply because sometimes things were so bad she actually didn't care.

Lucy came to a decision inside herself. "I can still like Claire without liking the way she acts. And I certainly don't have to join in with what she does!"

Gradually, Lucy helped Claire realize that drugs and shoplifting were only making things worse — that she had other choices. Claire had always liked swimming; Lucy persuaded her to learn to dive. Claire turned out to have quite a talent for it. Here was risk, and energy expenditure too, but it made her feel good about herself, rather than terrible! And Claire discovered that her mom coped a lot better with life when she helped her out rather than gave her extra grief.

Things improved for Claire, and she and Lucy stayed friends. But Lucy never forgot that her first responsibility was to herself — to Lucy. When Claire got in with a gang of real wasters, Lucy bowed right out. Claire knew that she could contact Lucy again when she wanted to. And she did.

SHOULD I HELP?

Claire was lucky, having a friend like Lucy. Lucy knew that there was more to Claire than the way she behaved sometimes, and she liked her enough to want to help.

Lucy was sensible to put herself first, though. Her mother needn't have worried. Claire didn't have a bad influence on Lucy — Lucy had a good one on Claire.

But it could have been the other way around. Lucy was able to help Claire because underneath Claire wanted to change. But some people don't want to change — either because they haven't really got the strength, or because they just don't want to.

The point at which you should stop trying to help someone is the point at which you feel it's harming YOU. Don't be bullied into staying in a destructive friendship, or made to feel guilty about "abandoning" someone who's trying to drag you down with them.

Some people are so messed up by what's happened to them in the past that they're beyond the help of their friends. They need professional help. Putting someone in touch with a caring or counseling organization might be the best act of friendship you could make.

LIFE IN THE FAMILY, LIFE IN THE WORLD

You're growing up now. One day, you will leave home — you probably already spend far less time there than when you were younger. More than likely, you see your friends a lot more than you see your parents.

THERE'S NO PLACE LIKE HOME

But home is still where you live. And the family is what you come back to. If you're lucky, your parents will understand that you're growing up. They will see that you need to be out and about, but that you also need a base, somewhere secure to come home to (and they won't shout "You treat this house like a hotel!" more than once a day...!).

But don't take your family too much for granted. Remember that while you are going through new experiences, starting to learn more both about yourself and the world around you, your parents need to get used to the "new" you. Take the time to talk to your parents.

Think, too, about your place in the family, what you can give back to it. You have a role to play here, just as you do in the world outside. Living in your family helps prepare you for that world: you learn the importance of sharing and accepting responsibilities, the need for some kind of order and the art of give and take. You absorb attitudes, values, and ways of behavior from your family. As you grow older, you can decide what attitudes and values you want to keep, and what you want to change.

Family life - what part do you play in yours?

ASSORTED FAMILIES — ASSORTED HELP

* Maybe yours is a chaotic family, people coming and going, things happening all the time. Enjoy the variety and offer to cook everyone a meal!

* Maybe it's a very organized family. Both parents are working, tight schedules are needed to get everything done. Try not to throw a wrench in the works too often. If things run smoothly, you stand to benefit as much as anyone else.

* Maybe it's a little family — just you and someone else. You and the person who cares for you have a special relationship — but you must both recognize the need for other relationships, too.

WHEN IT ALL GOES WRONG

Sometimes things in the family don't run smoothly. Most families go through difficult patches, and usually these bad times pass. But sometimes they create permanent change. Crisis times can make you feel betrayed. You feel your secure base has gone. You want to worry about school, friends, spots — not this. But you *can* cope.

WHEN PARENTS SEPARATE

There is no way around it, this can be a terrible time. Parents get locked into their own unhappiness and can neglect to talk to you. Often they think they're protecting you by keeping you in the dark. There may be arguing and bitterness — maybe one parent wants you to "take sides" against the other. Sometimes, when families are in crisis, you need to seek outside help. It is important to talk to someone about what you're going through. Try not to feel guilty. Children are almost never the cause of a breakup: strong marriages can withstand just about anything the offspring throw at them! Try not to take sides — they're still both your parents, and you probably want to continue seeing both of them.

Mom — I need to talk about you and Dad splitting up.

Of course, darling. What's on your mind?

Well, will we have to move?

I don't know. Look — that's not important. What matters is...

I mean — will I have to change schools?

I don't know! That's for the future! Right now...

Because I WON'T. I'm NOT moving!

Is that all you can think about, Sally? When my life's falling apart? You're so SELFISH!

Is Sally selfish? Or just concerned about her own survival? Maybe you think her mom's selfish. Or are they both just... human?

A TIME TO GRIEVE

The death of someone close to you is a terrible blow. It's like being wounded. You must accept that you'll need time to heal. Talk about the person who died, keep some mementos if you like — remembering is part of the healing process.

Unhappily, your friends may be embarrassed and even avoid you. They don't realize that you'd appreciate them making contact, however clumsily. Difficult as it may be at this time, you might have to ask them for their company. If you feel you need to, don't hesitate to seek outside help from counselors or support groups.

Sometimes, something good can come out of crisis times. Perhaps you take on new responsibilities and gain confidence as you learn to cope. As you draw closer to other people in your need for support, the bonds between you may deepen and strengthen.

GROUP OR GANG?

Teenagers like to group together. Large or small groups, fixed or flexible groups — it's happening all the time. They like doing the same things, going to the same places. They dress alike, act alike, listen to the same music.

But why is being part of a group so important? Why do we feel good and confident when we're in with our friends, and unhappy and inadequate if we're left out?

LIFE IN THE SWAMP

In primeval times, your very survival depended on being part of a tribe. To be excluded from the tribe was to die. Tribes had a strong outward identity and a strict internal order. And when your tribe fought another tribe, it had to win.

Could that be why we've got this instinct to "gang" up? How much do you think we've progressed from those old tribal days? In what ways are we still stuck back in the primordial swamp?

Read William Golding's book *Lord of the Flies* for a story of tribalism and a gang that gets frighteningly out of control!

"Some people call us a gang. There wouldn't be much point being with us if you didn't play football and spend most of your time talking about it." Max, age 13

"Yeah, there's about ten of us. We hang out together. We don't go looking for trouble, but we look out for each other." Jan, age 14

"No, it's not a gang. It's not that fixed. It's like a group of friends. Last week it was my birthday, and they all got together and gave me a party for a surprise. It was great!" Parvin, age 14

A GANGLAND MEMBER?

Being part of a group can be huge fun: you're sure of company, sure of something to do and with people who share your interests. And when your sense of self is still forming, it's good to feel you belong somewhere. But some groups aren't fun. If a gang's identity depends on those it excludes — even on those it attacks — that's a lot less healthy. It can lead to bullying, persecution, racism — all that. In bad gangs, the stronger members prey on the weaker. Younger members can be pushed into crime, drug use or dealing, just to keep up with the others. And if gang fighting breaks out, they can get hurt — even killed.

CASE HISTORY

The kids from the Belling complex stuck together. No one messed them around.

Then one of them, Corey, started turning up less often. He'd just shrug when they asked him where he'd been. The rest didn't like that; they confronted him. It's quite scary being confronted by seven blokes. "Look," Corey said, "I want to do some other things. I'm doing that film course at school. You get to see all these movies — they're excellent — and there just isn't time..."

"Hold on! You're either with us or you're not!" sneered one of the group.

But the others thought about it and said Corey should hang out when he could. "We have to be flexible," they said. "Things change."

Not long afterward one of the group started dating a girl, and he was around less often too. But he stayed in touch, like Corey. And finally, all the guys left school and did their different things — but they stayed friends for years.

PEER PRESSURE

There's nothing wrong with the feeling you get from being with a group of friends — it's great. But in that group, you still need to think for yourself. Be on your guard against pressure to do something you don't really want to. Watch out for "group decision."

Luckily, things have changed since those bad old days in the swamp: if you go against the tribe, you WILL survive. Sometimes you may need to go against the tribe TO survive. Make up your own mind on how you want to behave.

GROUP PSYCHOSIS

UNDER PRESSURE

If you've ever been the victim of bullying, you know just how destructive it can be. The very sight of the bully makes you feel sick, and you're constantly scared, waiting for the next assault. You feel helpless, worthless; you may even start to think there's something wrong with you, that the bully is in some way justified in picking on you.

There's no doubt about it, being bullied plays havoc with your self-esteem.

TAKE ACTION

Bullies tend to single you out for "differences" — your color, your height, your cleverness. Let's state something obvious here. Being bullied *is not your fault*! It is nothing to feel bad or guilty about. But if it goes on and on, it will start to damage you. If a bully is making your life an ordeal, you must seek help.

Some schools now have a definite bullying policy, with perhaps a specific teacher to go to. Bringing bullying out in the open works because bullying absolutely depends on the victim's silence. That silence helps the bully — it's going along with the crime. Don't be a victim — SPEAK OUT!

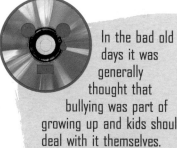

In the bad old days it was generally thought that bullying was part of growing up and kids should deal with it themselves. This is no longer the case!

WHY DO PEOPLE BULLY?

People bully others for all kinds of reasons. Because it makes them feel powerful, the center of attention. Because it gives them a thrill. Because it's the only way they can relate to people.

Maybe they've learned how to bully from being bullied themselves — and it's what they do to stop feeling so small inside.

If you're a bully, stand back and take a look at what you're doing. Are you really happy with how you are? You might be able to frighten people into being nice to you, but that's not the same as having friends. You might feel big, but only because you've made others feel small.

Imagine yourself in your victim's place. Bullies have driven people over the edge — to depression, to anorexia, to suicide. Will you be happy with yourself if you've been the cause of something like that? And bullying tends to spiral. You become immune to what you're doing, it seems normal and it gets worse and worse. Bullies can have all kinds of grief in adult life too — failed relationships, failed careers, even prison records. Change your behavior now before it wrecks everything.

SEXUAL BULLYING

If someone tries to pressure you to have sex when you don't want to, that's bullying, too. Don't give in to it! Sex isn't going to go away if you don't grab it at the first opportunity.

It's one of the good things in life. It's worth taking trouble over and waiting until you are ready emotionally. And it's certainly worth sharing with someone you really care for!

"BULLYING IN THE FAMILY IS A CONTRADICTION IN TERMS"

True or false? False, unfortunately. Bullying CAN happen in families. The usual rough and tumble of sibling and family life can sometimes take a much nastier turn. When this happens, try to insist your parents acknowledge it and deal with it. Seek outside help if need be. Sometimes parents themselves can be bullies physically or verbally. That can be very destructive because they really do have power over you. They should be caring for you, but they're hurting you.

If you are being abused, you must get help. Talk to an adult you trust, or call a helpline. Adult involvement is almost always necessary, both to stop the abuse and to help you recover.

And remember — it is NEVER a child's fault that he or she is being abused. Abuse is ALWAYS wrong.

ABUSE CAN TAKE FOUR DIFFERENT FORMS:

1. Physical — hitting, kicking — acts that can cause physical harm.
2. Emotional — taunts, sarcasm, verbal cruelty, no feeling of love in the home.
3. Neglect — where your physical needs (food, clothes, warmth) are not provided for.
4. Sexual — where someone forces you to take part in sexual activity. This can range from looking at pornographic videos to intercourse.

PROUD BUT NOT PREJUDICED

Pride in yourself doesn't mean you have to look down on other people. When you're sure of who you are, and happy with who you are, you have no need to belittle anyone to make yourself feel big. You feel big anyway. If, on the other hand, you feel the need to sneer at people and put them down, it could be because doing that makes you feel better about yourself. Putting others down gives you a lift. When you think about it, that's a bit sad!

JUST A LITTLE RESPECT...

If you genuinely like and respect yourself, it's easy to respect others too, and be tolerant about their differences. And when you're open to the differences in people, the world becomes a far richer, more interesting place. Other people's lifestyles, other people's views on the world, can be fascinating and mind-broadening. It's a cliché — but a valid one — to say that life would be dead dull if we were all the same!

However, when you're still making up your mind about where you fit into the world, it's tempting to buy wholesale into some group of ideas, or way of behaving. It helps you feel part of something. That's fine. But don't be narrow and lazy in your thinking. Don't take the easy way out by believing that anyone not into your type of life is inferior.

CASE HISTORY

Richard and Jason were very different. Richard was tall and strong and a great swimmer. Jason was small and wiry and he played chess at championship level. Richard couldn't imagine anything more boring than being stuck behind a board moving chess pieces around, and Jason just couldn't see the attraction of endlessly plunging into a cold pool. But they recognised the passion that each had for his chosen pastime, and they shared the same weird sense of humor. They got along great together.

Then Mark appeared on the scene. He was into swimming, too. He liked Richard a lot. But he couldn't stand Jason. "He's pathetic," Mark told Richard, "a total geek. What d'you want to hang around with him for?"

Pretty soon, Richard told Mark just where to go. "I like the way Jason's different," he said. "It's... refreshing. I don't want clones as friends."

There's room in your life for lots of different people. They don't all have to be like you. Are you open minded enough to respect what they do — and enjoy the variety that's around?

CASE HISTORY

Recently the principal of a very crowded Catholic school was begged by a Muslim mother to find a place for her son. The principal was puzzled by her enthusiasm for the school.

"But why is it so important for him to come here?" she asked. "We have such strong links with our church — maybe he'd be happier somewhere more neutral?"

The reply was emphatic: "You have such respect for your religion, that I know you'll respect mine too."

STEREOTYPING: A FORM OF PREJUDICE

Can you remember how you hated it when you were a child and some wacky aunt would say, "Oh, yes, here's Greg – he's the BRAINY one," or, "This is my little Sue — she loves animals?" You could walk in and kick the cat, but she'd still have you down as the "one who loves animals."

Well, that's stereotyping for you. People put other people in a pigeonhole, a box with a label, and they won't let them out again. It's another form of easy, lazy thinking. It's frustrating to be stereotyped. It's as if people can't see who you really are – just their wonky picture of you.

If you insist on thinking that all the kids from *that* complex are louts, or all the girls from *that* school are stuck up, your efforts toward them will end there. Is that how you want to be?

Don't limit others by having a narrow view of what they can or can't do.

Consider this remark by Sir James Dewar (the Scottish physicist): "Minds are like parachutes. They only function when they are open." Good, eh?

If you love heavy metal, will you despise someone who likes Beethoven? Or will you respect the fact that they, like you, have lots of music in their life?

BEYOND BLACK AND WHITE

Why do some groups need to attack others in order to feel good about themselves? From football fans to political parties, the drive for groups to pit themselves against other people is strong.

ORDER PLEASE!

As long as opposing groups are evenly matched, and the rules of contest are respected, maybe not too much harm is done. A real danger arises, however, when one group is a lot weaker, and the rules are ignored. What should have been a fair contest then becomes a riot.

MEANWHILE, BACK IN SWAMPLAND...

Something even more sinister happens when the fight is not about what you believe, but about what you ARE. In that lies the roots of racism, sexism and all the other "isms." People are condemned not for what they've done or said, but for whether they're black or white, male or female, or for their religion or nationality — and that's crazy.

If we look back at life in the primordial swamp again, we can understand how it came about: any individual who looked different would be considered a threat and not be accepted into a tribe. But is that really relevant today? Haven't we evolved a little?

THE SCAPEGOAT

Originally, a scapegoat was a real goat, symbolically laden with the sins of the Israelites, and sent out into the wilderness to its death. Today, we use the term to describe anyone who is blamed for things that have gone wrong. A scapegoat is a very comforting thing to have when times are bad. It means you have someone to direct all your anger against, and it means you don't have to use your brain much.

Hitler used the idea of the scapegoat to terrifying effect. After World War I, Germany was suffering severe economic depression. Hitler and his Nazi party harnessed the bitterness and anger in the country and directed it against the Jews and other minority groups. Hitler encouraged people to think that there was high unemployment because the Jews had taken all the jobs.

BROADMINDED?

Fighting ignorance really does help kill prejudice. Once you begin to find out about people, to see them as individuals, it's hard to dismiss them *en masse*. And maybe if you know something about their lives, you can begin to understand their behavior — even if you don't agree with it.

In today's world, it's more important than ever to look at people's deeds and words — not their race, religion, sex, or appearance!

COMBATING RACISM

ACTIVE racism is a particularly nasty form of bullying. The rules for combating bullying also apply to dealing with racism. Go to teachers at school and complain. Inform the police if necessary: racial harassment is a criminal offense.

PASSIVE racism — looks, sneers, coldness — is harder to deal with directly. Rather than argue back, which is what the bully wants you to do, use a technique called "fogging." Imagine yourself surrounded by banks of thick, protective fog. The words are swallowed up: they don't reach you. Try to see the bully's behavior as his or her problem — not yours.

More sinister yet, according to the Nazis these groups did not belong to the "master race": they had the wrong color hair and eyes, the wrong religion. They became the scapegoat for all that was wrong with Germany. Hitler's ideas resulted in more than 6 million Jewish people and people of other minority groups being killed in concentration camps during World War II.

STRONG, NOT SELFISH...

We all know people who are like monsters of selfishness, who think they're the only one who matters. They've made "looking out for Number One" into a creed for survival. The thing is, survival is just about all they achieve — certainly not life as we know it! It might look as though such people are in charge and getting what they want from life, but if their concerns stop at Number One, they've shut the door on interaction, development, emotions — all the things that give life its juice. People who care only about themselves have something dead about them.

MIDDLE GROUND?

And perhaps you also know a few people who are the opposite, people who don't appear to think they matter at all. People who always give, give, give, with no thought for their own needs or wishes. They always go along with the crowd and never stick up for what they want.

So where's the middle ground? How can you be strong, but not selfish — kind, but not a pushover?

SAY 'YES', SAY 'NO'?

If someone asks you to do them a favor, what's your response? Is it an automatic "No" because you refuse to be taken advantage of? Or is it an equally automatic "Yes," because...well, you're just nice like that?

Or is it because you DARE NOT say no? One secret in getting the right balance is to stand back from the situation. Try to be like a judge weighing the pros and cons, seeing both sides. That way you'll make sure that when you say yes or no, it's for the right reasons.

And when you're weighing it, don't forget to add to the "yes" side of the scales the pleasure that comes from doing someone a good turn!

CONSIDER THIS...

Your friend asks you to get her some gerbil food from town. She says she's too busy to go in herself. If you're thinking of going in anyway, and your friend is great and does you favors (and you like playing with her gerbils!), you might well say "yes."

If you've got stacks of homework to do and, anyway, your friend didn't pay you back for the gerbil food you bought her last time until you'd reminded her three times, you might well say "no — get it yourself!"

SEVERAL RIGHT ANSWERS

A REASONABLE REFUSAL

Mom, don't you remember? I've got tickets for that new band, Mirage! I CAN'T watch him tonight!

A FEEL-GOOD YES

But it's EASY! OK – sit down. I'll show you.

Rashid – you're a hero.

MATHS

A COMPROMISE

Jane, NO! It's my best shirt, and I'M wearing it tonight. You can borrow my green one.

OK. OK. I should be assertive. But I'm not. I go into victim mode and everyone walks all over me. I can't change what I am inside

Assertiveness is a skill that comes into all walks of life. It will keep you from being overlooked, pushed around, or pushed into things you want to steer clear of.

But you can ACT as though you have changed! Make eye contact, breathe slowly, pretend to be in control. People will start to treat you as an assertive person... and you'll be on the way to becoming one!

23

RESTRICT OR PROTECT?

Rules, rules, rules. They seem to multiply as you get older, tying you down, caging you in. The trick in coping with the idea of rules or laws is to see them as protecting, not restricting, you. If most people agree to follow them, people have freedom within a workable structure. Rules actually protect your rights.

WHAT WOULD HAPPEN IF...?

Imagine what would happen if there were no rules on the roads. No one would have to drive safely. There'd be instant mass carnage!

There's a question that adults tend to bleat at you if you drop a candy wrapper or something: "What would happen if everyone did that?" Well, what would happen? If everyone threw down garbage, if everyone smashed things up, or if everyone shoplifted? What would happen if everyone could do what they wanted, however and whenever they felt like it, to whoever and whatever they chose?

It might feel good for a while, but only until YOU started getting attacked, or stolen from, or run over. People need some sort of organization to survive. A land without laws would rapidly turn into mass destructive chaos, where the strong prey on the weak.

But we were just having a little FUN! Too much to ask, is it? Me and my friends were going along, singing and pushing each other around a bit, and first this woman screams at us that we woke up her baby, and then this man has a go at us cuz Mike fell on his car.

Then, on top of all that, this old lady tells us off 'cos we dropped a couple of cans — I mean EXCUSE US FOR BREATHING!

Point taken. But your freedom encroached on their rights — that's why they complained!

Exciting on celluloid — but would you really want to LIVE there?

LAWS: A CLOSER LOOK

Society isn't only concerned with laws to control kids! Most countries have laws to protect them, too. These laws are concerned with the rights and welfare of children. If you are being abused or neglected, the authorities will step in to ensure your safety, and to make sure your abuser is punished.

Laws about under-age sex or drinking are there for your protection, too. Anyone who has sexual intercourse with a child under the age of sixteen is liable to prosecution. Anyone selling cigarettes or alcohol to someone under the age of twenty-one is also liable to prosecution: the law recognizes that alcohol is especially harmful to a growing young person, and in some countries manufacturers must include a health warning when cigarettes are sold as these are harmful at any age!

The tough laws against the use of drugs such as heroin and cocaine are also to protect you. Penalties for selling illegal drugs are extremely severe, and governments spend huge amounts of money trying to catch drug dealers and suppliers. They know how these drugs can destroy people — physically, emotionally, and socially.

I have to say, I think our artwork beats yours... but then we did have a lot longer to do it in...

STEALING

You may think that, with all the inequalities around, stealing is one way of evening out the balance. But are things really so bad for you that you feel you have to steal to survive? If you start to thieve, you put yourself partly outside society's protection, because you've broken society's rules. It's no fun to be in trouble with the police. It's also worth thinking — how would it feel if it happened to you? If someone went off with your bike, your money, your coat? If you commit crimes, do you really deserve to be protected from the crimes of other people?

LIFE ON THE EDGE?

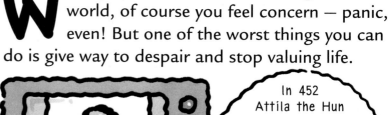

Well, I don't care – about laws or society or anything else. Nothing works! Look at the state everything's in. Stockpiled weapons – enough to destroy the world a hundred times over. Diseases. Pollution. Fear on the streets. Unemployment. What's the point?

When you look at all that is wrong with the world, of course you feel concern — panic, even! But one of the worst things you can do is give way to despair and stop valuing life.

In 452 Attila the Hun swept through Europe, devastating all before him.... By the end of 1348, one-third of the population of Europe had died from the Black Death.... During the Industrial Revolution children as young as six were working long hours down mines and in factories....

HAS IT EVER BEEN ANY DIFFERENT?

The truth is, life is no more difficult now than it ever was. In many ways it's a lot easier. It just depends on what events you focus on. Buying into the "doom and gloom" view is comforting in a bleak sort of way, because you don't have to try. You can give up — before you've even started!

But you *can* make a difference. You can change things, however small. Start with yourself — the center of your world. Protect yourself, care for yourself. Move out into the sphere of your family and friends. How can you make things better there? Then consider your

community, and the world at large. You have a role to play in all of it. As we saw at the beginning of the book, small things are important. They lead on to other things — they have an accumulative effect.

"All that is needed for evil to triumph, is for good people to do nothing."

Helping out is a two-way process.

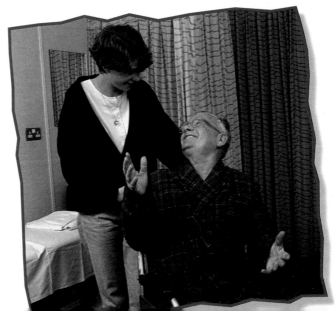

Rhino horn is worth three times the price of gold. Removing the horn from this rhino will protect it from being killed by poachers.

⚙ People power: Public opinion has meant that big businesses and politicians have had to take on board the Green Message. Now we can buy organic meats and vegetables, lead-free gasoline, biodegradable detergents, but it doesn't stop there...

⚙ Recycle/Reuse: Landfills for garbage are running out of space and the supply of natural materials such as wood and oil is becoming depleted. Recycling things is becoming more important. Even better is the reuse of materials, since this uses even less energy than the recycling process.

⚙ Walk, don't drive: Every time you walk, cycle or use public transport somewhere instead of getting into the car, you're helping the health of both you and the environment.

ENVIRONMENTAL ANGST

Scary stories about the thinning of the ozone layer and global warming always seem to be in the news. So do disturbing stories about the destruction of the rain forests and of animals in danger. It's easy to feel despair. What are we doing to our planet?

Or, what SHOULD we be doing?

Once again, it's a message of small things adding up. Every time you think "who cares, it's too late anyway," and lob an empty coke can in the bushes, you're adding to the down side. Every time you take that coke can somewhere to be recycled, you're adding to the up side. It's that simple.

Have a good look around your neighborhood. Is there somewhere you could plant trees, clean up, make a change for the better?

You and the world are precious. Take great care of both!

IT'S YOUR LIFE

It takes time to discover exactly who you are and what you want from life. It takes time to realize your potential, to grow into who you're going to be. You're still on the way there, and that's fine. It's an important journey you're making; take all the time you need!

REALIZING YOUR POTENTIAL

The French have a saying to describe someone who's happy with who he or she is: "Il est bien dans sa peau" — "he fits his skin!" Sounds great, doesn't it? But right now, half the time you probably don't feel ANYTHING fits!

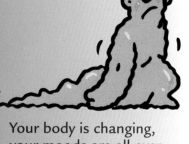

Your body is changing, your moods are all over the place. You're caught between wanting to be independent, and being nervous of what lies in front of you. It's not surprising you sometimes feel lost and confused.

Take a big breath, and think about what's inside your skin — that miracle, your body. It's a good place to start. You might not be as tall or as thin or as strong as you'd like, but if you are healthy, you're very lucky.

IT'S BASIC

Your body is amazing. But if it's not treated well it won't flourish. The truth is very simple. If you eat well and exercise regularly, you have a good chance of keeping fit and feeling great. But if you eat nothing but junk food, you will probably feel and look pretty grim. And if you regularly poison your body with alcohol, cigarettes, drugs, and inhalants, your body — and your mind — won't flourish. They will start to go downhill. Fast.

If you treated a car like some people treat their bodies, and poured junk and poisons into its gas tank, no one would be a bit surprised if it ground to a halt and fell to pieces!

CARING FOR YOU

It makes sense to consider just how much personal control you have in the way you treat your body. You've almost certainly got more influence than anyone else! Although it can be hard to take a stand when everyone around you appears to be set in slob- or self-destruct mode, it is possible! And when you start to feel better and better, and life gets richer and richer, you'll find it easy to stick to treating your body well!

CHOICES

You're the one in charge of your life. You're the one who's in control. Ultimately, it's up to you. You make so many decisions, every day: when to say yes, when to say no, when to take part, when to walk away. Increasingly in your life, you make decisions that affect you and the people around you.

WHO WILL YOU BE?

You have choice here, too. Some people are like drains — they take and take, draining the energy from those around them, but they're never full, never satisfied. "Drains" are not happy people — and they're not fun to be around.

Other people are like radiators — they give off warmth and positive feelings. They attract people; and the warmth they give off tends to radiate back to them. "Radiators" see life as a two-way process: you get out of life what you put into it.

Will you work to make things better, for you and the people around you? Which would you rather be — a drain or a radiator?

WHAT WILL YOU DO?

Consider your options carefully. Don't just go with the crowd; don't let anyone push you into things or rush you into things. You're making choices for yourself and the life ahead of you, and this life isn't a rehearsal — it's the only one you've got. Make sure you start out on the life you want to lead. And remember to enjoy the journey!

Will you let life just happen to you — or set out to lead the life you want to live? Growing and changing into the person you want to be is one of the most exciting things in life!

LETTER FROM LIFE EDUCATION

Dear Friends:

The first Life Education Center was opened in Sydney, Australia, in 1979. Founded by the Rev. Ted Noffs, the Life Education program came about as a result of his many years of work with drug addicts and their families. Noffs realized that preventive education, beginning with children from the earliest possible age all the way into their teenage years, was the only long-term solution to drug abuse and other related social problems.

Life Education pioneered the use of technology in a "Classroom of the 21st Century," designed to show how drugs, including nicotine and alcohol, can destroy the delicate balance of human life. In every Life Education classroom, electronic displays show the major body systems, including the respiratory, nervous, digestive and immune systems. There is also a talking brain, a wondrous star ceiling, and Harold the Giraffe, Life Education's official mascot. Programs start in preschool and continue through high school.

Life Education also conducts parents' programs including violence prevention classes, and it has also begun to create interactive software for home and school computers.

There are Life Education Centers operating in seven countries (Thailand, the United States, the United Kingdom, New Zealand, Australia, Hong Kong, and New Guinea), and there is a Life Education home page on the Internet (the address is http://www.lec.org/).

If you would like to learn more about Life Education International contact us at one of the addresses listed below or, if you have a computer with a modem, you can write to Harold the Giraffe at Harold@lec.org and you'll find out that a giraffe can send E-mail!

Let's learn to live.

All of us at the Life Education Center.

Life Education, USA
149 Addison Ave
Elmhurst, Illinois
60126
Tel: 630 530 8999
Fax: 630 530 7241

Life Education, UK
20 Long Lane
London
EC1A 9HL
United Kingdom

Life Education,
Australia
PO Box 1671
Potts Point
NSW 2011
Australia

Life Education,
New Zealand
126 The Terrace
PO Box 10-769
Wellington
New Zealand

GLOSSARY

Abuse To use or treat someone or something in a way that is wrong and will cause serious harm.

Assertive Someone who speaks out for what he/she believes, and is not put off by the opinions of others. Being assertive does not mean being loud or rude; quiet determination is almost always far more effective.

Attila the Hun Leader of a tribe of nomadic Asian horsemen who invaded the Middle East and much of the Roman Empire in A.D. 451 and 452.

Black Death The deadly plague (probably bubonic) that reached Europe from Asia in the mid-fourteenth century. Thousands of people died of it. The last outbreak of plague in Britain was in the seventeenth century.

Celluloid A type of plastic used for movie film.

Cliché A much-used phrase or idea; one that is not original.

Clone An organism that is identical in every way with another organism. (This is not the case with identical twins.)

Counselor Someone who gives advice and help.

Fogging A good way to deal with bullying and any verbal harassment: imagine you are surrounded by thick fog banks that blot out all sound. Get your imagination going as soon as it's obvious that someone is going to try to bully you. It also helps if you keep reminding yourself that bullies are often weak, inadequate people – in character if not in size!

Group psychosis In medical terms, psychosis occurs when someone with mental problems loses touch with reality. Group psychosis occurs when a group of people, such as a crowd in a sports stadium, gets out of control and causes trouble. The group has lost touch with reality, although as individuals away from the crowd they would be unlikely to act out and almost certainly do not suffer from mental problems.

Harassment When someone purposely scares or threatens another person; subjects them to repeated attacks.

Nazi party The German National Socialist party of which Adolf Hitler became the leader in the 1930s. A feature of the party was the way it made hatred of certain races and religions an important part of its beliefs.

Peer pressure Pressure applied by a group of people of similar age, interests or status. Peer pressure is not necessarily obvious, or negative.

Philosopher Someone who studies ideas and thinks about human behavior and the meaning of life.

Prejudice An opinion, usually unpleasant, held by someone who knows little about the subject or person concerned.

Primeval Relating to the time when the Earth was formed.

Primordial Existing at or belonging to the time when the Earth was formed.

Stereotype A person or thing that conforms to a fixed mental picture or idea that is usually incorrect because it has taken no account of individuality.

FURTHER INFORMATION

These organizations can help you with your questions:

American Humane Association Children's Division
63 Inverness Drive E
Englewood, CO 80112-5117
Tel: (303) 792-9900
    (800) 227-4645

Child Welfare League of America
440 1st Street NW
Suite 310
Washington, DC 20001
Tel: (202) 638-2952

Friends of the Earth
1025 Vermont Avenue NW
3rd Floor
Washington, DC 20005
Tel: (202) 783-7400

INDEX